nurture

50 TIPS

to **nourish** your
heart & soul

David & Heidi Cuschieri

Nurture: 50 tips to nourish your heart & soul
David Cuschieri, Heidi Cuschieri

1st ed.
ISBN 9780994252906 (pbk.)

Self-care, health, inspiration, wisdom, mental health.

Published by The Next Big Think
For further information about orders:
Email: info@the-next-big-think.com
Website: www.the-next-big-think.com

DISCLAIMER
We have made every effort to ensure the use of references contained in this book have been referenced correctly. If you believe an error has been made with regards to any of the references in this book, please contact us at:
info@the-next-big-think.com .

5O TIPS

to **nourish** your
heart & soul

GREETING BOOK SERIES
by David & Heidi Cuschieri

THE GREATEST LOVE STORY EVER

Contrary to scientific fact, we never really grow up. We grow up in the sense that we get bigger but we are still children at heart. You only need to ask elderly people - although their legs may not work as well as they used to they still feel young at heart.

Our bodies are constantly renewing themselves with old cells dying and new ones being formed to replace them. As we age the ability for cells to replicate exactly the same doesn't work so well. It is the nourishment in the food we provide ourselves and exercise that can help prolong our life. What is also important is lowering our stress levels. Our body and mind are infinitely connected and by nurturing ourselves holistically we can ensure our total well-being.

Life gifts us with many challenges that help us to grow. Some of these challenges can be overwhelming and having the skills and the support network of those around us can make all the difference in our recovery. We aren't robots, we are living feeling human beings but sometimes we may push ourselves too far. Unlike a car that we need to maintain through regular servicing, we aren't mechanical and need more than just a servicing, we need regular TLC. We each have a heart and soul that need to be nurtured with positive thoughts and surrounded with love.

Because we are children trapped in adult bodies we mustn't forget that our inner child needs to be carefully nurtured. Nurturing ourselves creates strong relationships with ourselves, others and the world around us. When we feel well-cared for, we are able to share ourselves with the world. This sharing of ourselves and our heart creates connection. Nurturing ourselves begins with stopping negative self-talk, the kind of unsupportive, self-defeating, abusive and self-prophesizing statements that end up becoming the reality we create for ourselves.

This life that we have is a special gift that we can use to learn, to be spontaneous, to love unconditionally, to open up our heart and mind to the wonder of the universe. Nurture your heart and learn to keep good thoughts and let go of negativity and be grateful for the good in your life. Solitude and meditation help us to reflect on life's lessons, develop wisdom and resilience, and helps us to reconnect again to ourselves and the world around us.

By truly loving yourself, you are able to connect with others from a deep heartfelt level. You are able to empathize with other people's pain, be more compassionate and come to the conclusion that life is all about love. Some of the most enlightened and happiest people are those who have found their passion in life and it is often related to serving others. It is a fact that when we give to others of ourselves we feel deep joy.

Nurturing others is just as important as caring for ourselves. We can do this everyday in little things to encourage growth and development, protect, and nourish those around us. Be an example for others. Be generous with your time and attention. Listen to them. Encourage others to see their greatness. Compliment them and be compassionate. We all have our own demons to face - help lighten their journey.

Nurture: 50 tips to nourish your heart & soul will provide you with ways to deeply connect with your inner-self and others in meaningful life affirming heart-felt ways. Through implementing the simple habits in this book you can create a life filled with joy, passion and deep connection and be able to share it with the ones you love.

To the greatest love story ever - you.

David and Heidi Cuschieri

SHARING
CARING

Spending time in nature can have a soothing effect on the soul.

Disconnecting from technology and re-connecting to nature

helps to re-balance us. Nature allows us to connect to the rhythm

of life and re-discover how interconnected we all are.

We are just as much a part of this living world as the animals and

plants around us.

IS

TIP #01

Whether it is having your lunch in a nearby park, a swim at the beach, or going for a

hike in the woods, regularly factor in nature nurture time to re-connect to Mother

Nature and allow her to re-energize your body and spirit.

UN
LIMITED

You are capable of greatness. You are only limited by your thoughts.

Some of the most successful people didn't let limited resources stop

them from great achievements as they had something within that was

more important than external circumstances - they had resourcefulness.

TIP #02

To achieve greatness, set yourself clear precise goals. Nurture positive thoughts.

Take conscious action, always holding true to your vision and you too will discover the

freedom that comes when you truly believe in your unlimited potential.

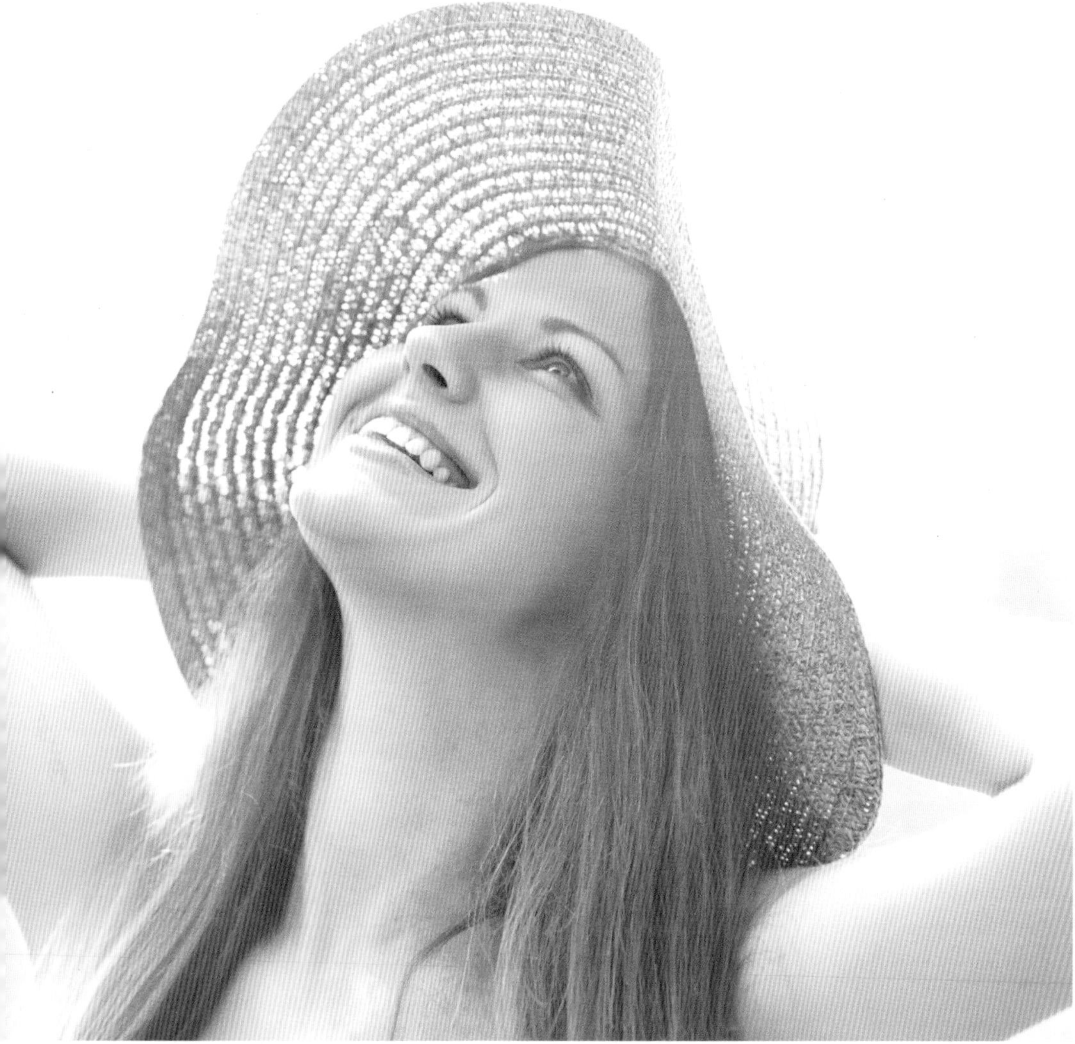

RE
LEASE

Have you ever noticed how weighed down and uptight you feel when you have been holding onto something? Then when you let go of the thought, situation or energy, you felt released almost as if you had been holding your breath for so long. Nourish yourself with positive thoughts.

TIP #03

For a new lease on life, ensure you regularly let go of any negativity, whether it be negative thoughts, toxic relationships, situations or emotions that don't add joy to your life. Just like your body, your mind needs regular flushing away of toxic thoughts that keep you down.

TIP
03

RELEASE

GIRL'S DAY OUT

A girl's day out is a wonderful way to break away from routine and responsibility, and let your hair down. Having great friends that you can feel free to just be yourself, laugh and be silly with is liberating.

TIP #04

Free yourself from the every day. Organize a Girl's Day Out. Go shopping or out to lunch at your favorite restaurant. It is your day to just be yourself amongst friends and create moments of connection that you all can cherish. Ensure you regularly roster GDO's into your schedule.

WORK OF HEART

The American mythologist and writer Joseph Campbell was famous

for the phrase "Follow your bliss". When you find your passion,

Campbell said, "doors will open where you didn't know they were

going to be". Whether it is your career or anything you do, let

passion be your compass.

TIP #05

Life is short. Too short to not be doing what you love for any period of time. Find what it is

that excites you to get up each morning . We spend a great part of our lives working so it is

important to love what you do so that your work becomes a work of heart.

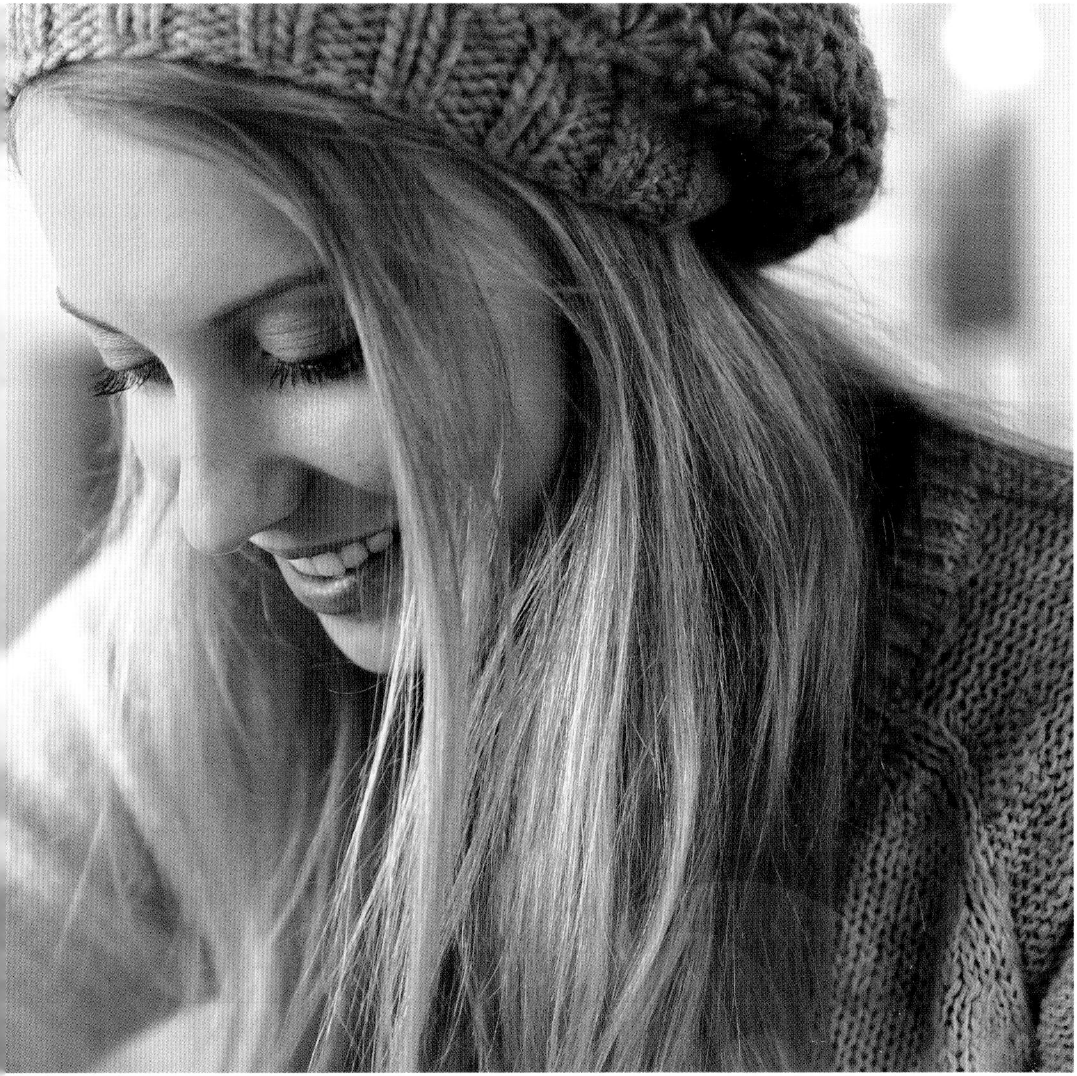

HEART
MADE

Hand-made gifts have a way of touching our hearts.

Knowing that someone we love has taken the time, thought and

effort to make us feel good, is a gift that no amount of money

could ever buy.

TIP #06

There is so much pleasure and enjoyment we can get from making others smile through

being thoughtful. Why not make a cake, a batch of cookies or a lovely little card to give to

those special people in your life and you will discover the infinite joy in giving.

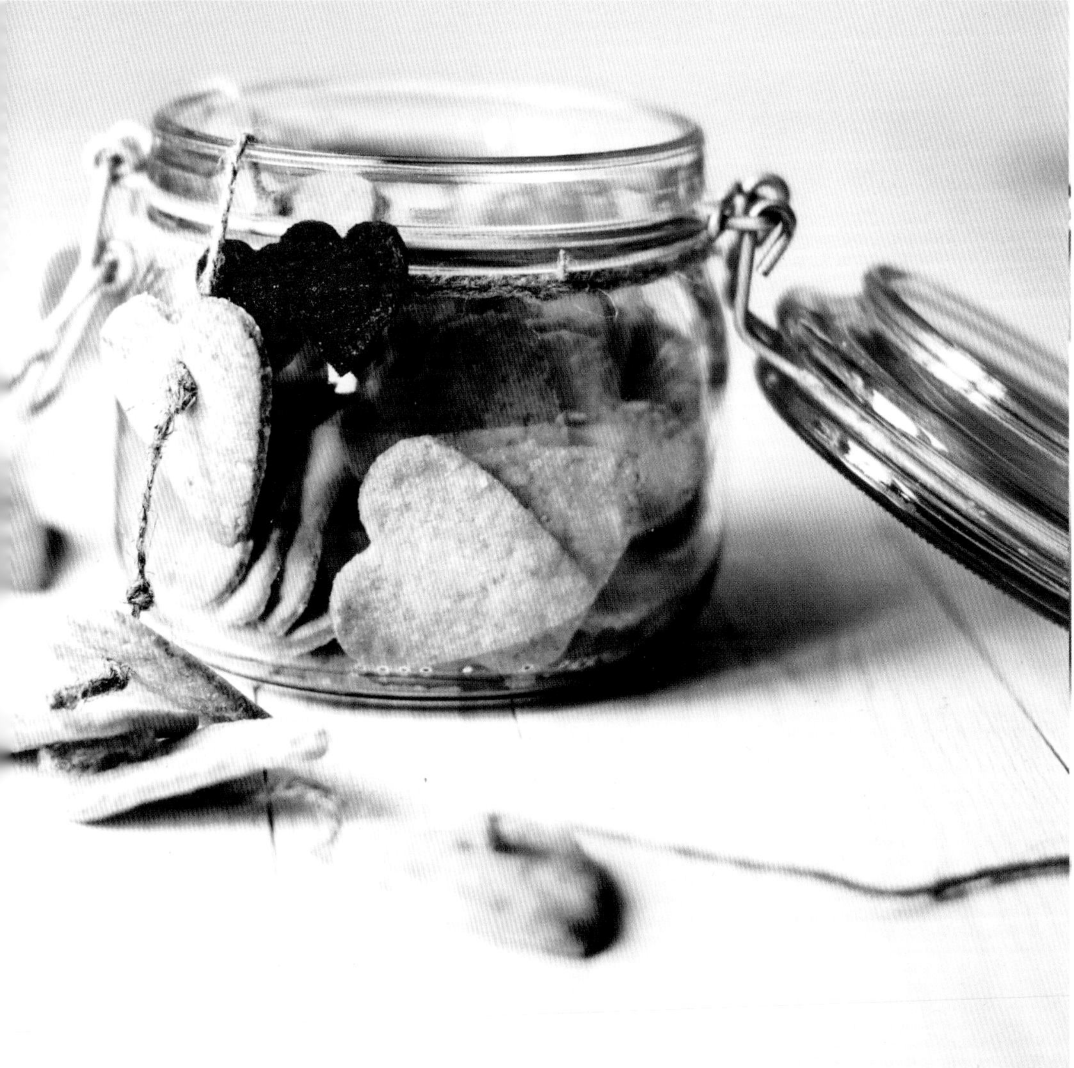

TIP 06 HEART MADE

HIGH
DIVE IT

Have you ever done something where you were nervous and felt your heart racing rapidly? Yet afterwards, the joy and energy you felt was exhilarating. Each time we dive higher we create a bigger splash out of our comfort zone.

TIP #07

High diving it or taking small steps out of your comfort zone, will help you expand and grow in confidence. Remember, every time you 'high dive it', remember to 'high five it' by celebrating your win.

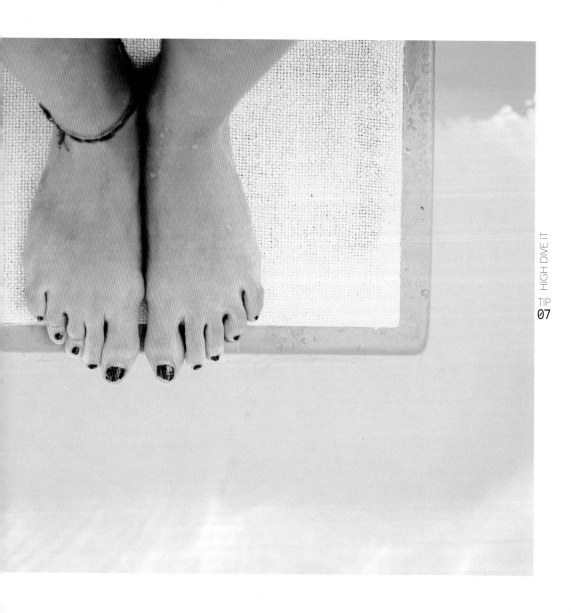

MUSE
IT

Music can have a nurturing effect on our heart and soul.

Listening to songs can trigger memories and make us feel

good. Music can relax us and relieve stress and anxiety.

Playing music brings out our inner muse and dancing to

it can make us feel alive. Listening to calming music can

assist us to sleep, relieve symptoms of depression and can

even induce in us a meditative or hypnotic state.

TIP #08

Make music part of your life to relax and uplift you. Let music's rhythm, melody and harmony soothe, inspire and move your soul.

WITH
COMPS

Don't ever underestimate the power that a kind word can have on others and also on you. Sincere praise makes people feel valued and appreciated. Showing your admiration and respect to others makes them feel good but it is this recognition of another that creates connection and joy within ourselves also.

TIP #09

Compliments when they are sincere and heartfelt can help build the receiver's self-esteem and make you feel good too. Commending or praising work colleagues on a job well done creates a happy working environment where people feel good.

MEMOR ISCING

Looking at old photos can bring us great joy as we look back at the good times and remember the people we shared them with along the way.

Memories are powerful and nostalgia can take us back to re-live the emotions we felt back in the 'good old days'. However, be careful to not let the past stop you from being present and color your experience of now.

TIP #10

Memories can have a powerful effect upon us. Reminiscing about the past can bring back the joy and energy we felt at that moment. Remembering the past by looking through old photographs of family and friends is a great way to uplift your soul.

CULT
URED

Have you ever gone to watch a play, a live theater production, a concert or a ballet performance? Dressing up and attending a live performance is a magical experience. It can transport your mind to another place, taking you away from the everyday.

TIP #11

Instead of going to the movies or shopping, why not organize to take in a bit of culture with friends. Make it a social night out, dress up, go to dinner and then head out to the live performance. Immerse yourself in music and the arts. Nurture your soul - be cultured.

RR
& R

They say that change is as good as a vacation so make sure you regularly

afford yourself time off from work and the everyday. Regular rest and

recreation will ensure that you maintain your health and happiness.

It gives you time to switch off your mind, exercise, and socialize.

TIP #12

It is more beneficial and often easier with our busy lives to give ourselves regular short breaks

to rest, recuperate, and 're-create' than having one extended break after a long stint of work.

Set aside 'me' time everyday, regardless if it is only a few minutes, where you can switch off.

Make the most of the weekends. Whenever you can go away on a mini-holiday.

SKY
HIGH

Looking up at the sky can literally uplift you or elevate your sense of well-being. We spend so much time these days with our heads down in thought and looking at our smart phones that we are often disconnected from the real world. Sky watching not only makes you look up, it also 'grounds' you in the present. Plus being in the sunshine helps to clear out the dark recesses of your mind.

TIP #13

Spending time regularly observing and appreciating nature's ever-shifting show can make

you feel 'sky high'. After all it is difficult to 'feel down' when we are literally 'looking up'.

KARMA
GARDENER

Gardening is an activity that can help relieve stress, making us feel calmer, provide us with wholesome nourishment and can even teach us about relationships. Whether you have a vegetable patch, a potted plant or an herb garden on your window sill, you will soon find out that when you tend to your plants with a little water and fertilizer they thrive, and when you neglect them they wither and die.

TIP #14

Let tending for plants teach you to become a karma gardener. Remember

that in any relationship it is what you sow that will determine what you reap.

FLOWER

Flowers have been revered as gifts since the beginning of time.

Their sensual beauty, color and fragrance have a grounding

effect upon us pulling us back into our body and out of our mind.

TIP #15

At home or at work, make sure that you always have flowers around you. When you are

feeling overwhelmed, enflower yourself. Simply have a flower nap from your thoughts by

taking in the beauty of the flower - inhale its calming fragrance, admire its exquisite

color, feel the softness of its petals and notice how it brightens up the room. Witness your

thoughts clear as you connect to your body and come back to your senses.

SET SAIL

Sometimes we can create unwanted stress and anxiety in our lives simply because we don't feel clear about where we are going in life. Uncertainty can make us feel mighty uncomfortable. Nothing in life is truly certain, but setting goals will help relieve the stress. You need to know where you are going to know when you have arrived and to do this you need to create a clear map.

TIP #16

Set clear achievable goals. Set sail by taking consistent action. Better to break up your main goal into smaller chunks with specific actions and celebrate these small wins along the way to keep the momentum and energy going.

destination

TREE

DOM

Buddha meditated under a Bodhi tree and attained enlightenment.
You too can experience a sense of enlightenment by spending
time around trees. Forests provide life to countless creatures,
food for us to eat, medicines to heal, clean air to breathe and
water to drink. Trees are nature's gift to us.

TIP #17

Spend time around trees. Go for a hike in a forest or a run in the local park, sit under
the shade of a tree and listen to the birds sing. Breathe in the fresh air they provide
and experience treedom.

LOVE
FEST

It is the little things, not the big gestures, that make life grand.

Breakfast in bed, a cup of coffee in the morning, making dinner,

a single rose, a hug - these are the little big things that make

life worth living.

TIP #18

Why not make breakfast in bed for your loved one. Pick a time, such as a Sunday, when

you both don't have to be anywhere in particular and surprise them. Little surprises

like these celebrate how much you love them and will be warmly appreciated.

GIVE
TIME

The greatest gift you can give another human being is your time.

Time to be present. Time to listen. Time to just be there.

Be generous with your time, it costs you nothing but it is priceless.

TIP #19

The relationships where we feel most nurtured are those where we feel heard.

Being fully present to others when they speak and not thinking what you are

going to say next, but just simply listening, is the greatest gift you can give.

LOVE LETTERS

Receiving thoughtful little sticky notes around the house from loved ones, or a special card in the mail from a good friend are the glue that keeps the relationships in our lives lovingly connected.

TIP #20

Don't wait for a special occasion to send a heart-felt message, whether it be by email, post-it note or greeting card. Let them know how grateful you are for having them in your life today.

The great thing about expressing your gratitude is that you *both* end up feeling great!

SOUL

ITUDE

Spending time on your own is very important in a world where we are constantly bombarded by information and demands on our time. Solitude gives you the chance to clear away distractions and reflect. It allows you the time to slow down, clear your cluttered mind and re-connect with yourself. It can also increase your creativity, concentration and productivity as it gives you time to think clearly and focus. Quiet time alone gives you the skills to not let your happiness be reliant on others and to enjoy things that *you* want to do.

TIP #21

Set aside regular 'me' time whether it be waking up early and going for a walk or meditating, or simply enjoying a cup of coffee with your cell phone turned off. Alone time will help you to re-energize and see things from a different perspective. Solitude is good for the soul.

INNER
WILD

It is arguable whether we ever truly grow up, and we are in fact simply children in adult sized bodies. One thing that is certain is that as adults our responsibilities increase with work, family and social commitments. It becomes easy to neglect your inner child. Learn to nurture your inner child and embrace activities that let you feel the freedom of childhood.

TIP #22

Do things that you enjoyed as a child or if you have children be fully present when you play with them. Be carefree and stop holding onto or obsessing over things that aren't really that important. Be spontaneous - climb a tree, jump over the cracks in the pavement, be wild again!

LOVE
YOU

One of the most selfish things you can do is to *not* love yourself.

It not only affects you but everyone around you who doesn't have the

opportunity to see just how incredible you really are. Remember that

you are totally unique. Be yourself. Love yourself. Let others see *you*.

TIP #23

Sometimes the greatest barrier to having a healthy self-esteem is the negative self-image we

have of ourself. Begin by not comparing yourself with others and instead write a list of the

things you like about yourself and that you are good at. Then ask those who you trust to tell

you what they like about you. Now focus on these points to create a positive self-image.

GIVE LIVE

Many feel that they don't know what they want to do with their lives.

Those people who are most passionate, are those who have found

their calling which is often centered around giving to others.

TIP #24

When we serve others it creates great joy and purpose in our lives. Whether you are a

mother, a school teacher, or a nurse knowing that you are helping others, is self-fulfilling.

If you aren't currently doing something fulfilling begin by thinking how you can use your

talents and abilities to serve others. It may mean learning new skills. When we are giving

of ourselves in some way we feel that we are living and not just *making a living*.

MEEDOM

Do you recognize the person staring back at you in the mirror?

Are you too eager to please others to fit in and be liked?

Do you feel that you cannot always be your authentic self and that

you need to adjust your invented self to fit in with different crowds?

It can be hard work keeping up appearances and not truly

being yourself. It also might be difficult to want to get to know

yourself fully. Self-discovery is a lifelong journey.

TIP #25

Get to know yourself through self observation and inquiry. Write down your values and

what things are important to you. Begin to operate from your core values, stop being too

eager to please, allow yourself to be yourself and you will discover true freedom.

HAPPY
MEDIUM

Just like a child on a swing our lives have high and low points.

That is life. Period. To remove suffering in our lives we first need

to understand what is causing the suffering. It is our thoughts.

When we are able to balance our thoughts we regain equanimity

or what we like to call 'the happy medium'.

TIP #26

When you are feeling stressed or anxious and under pressure, take a deep breath and

release the tension and negativity with your out breath to bring you back into balance.

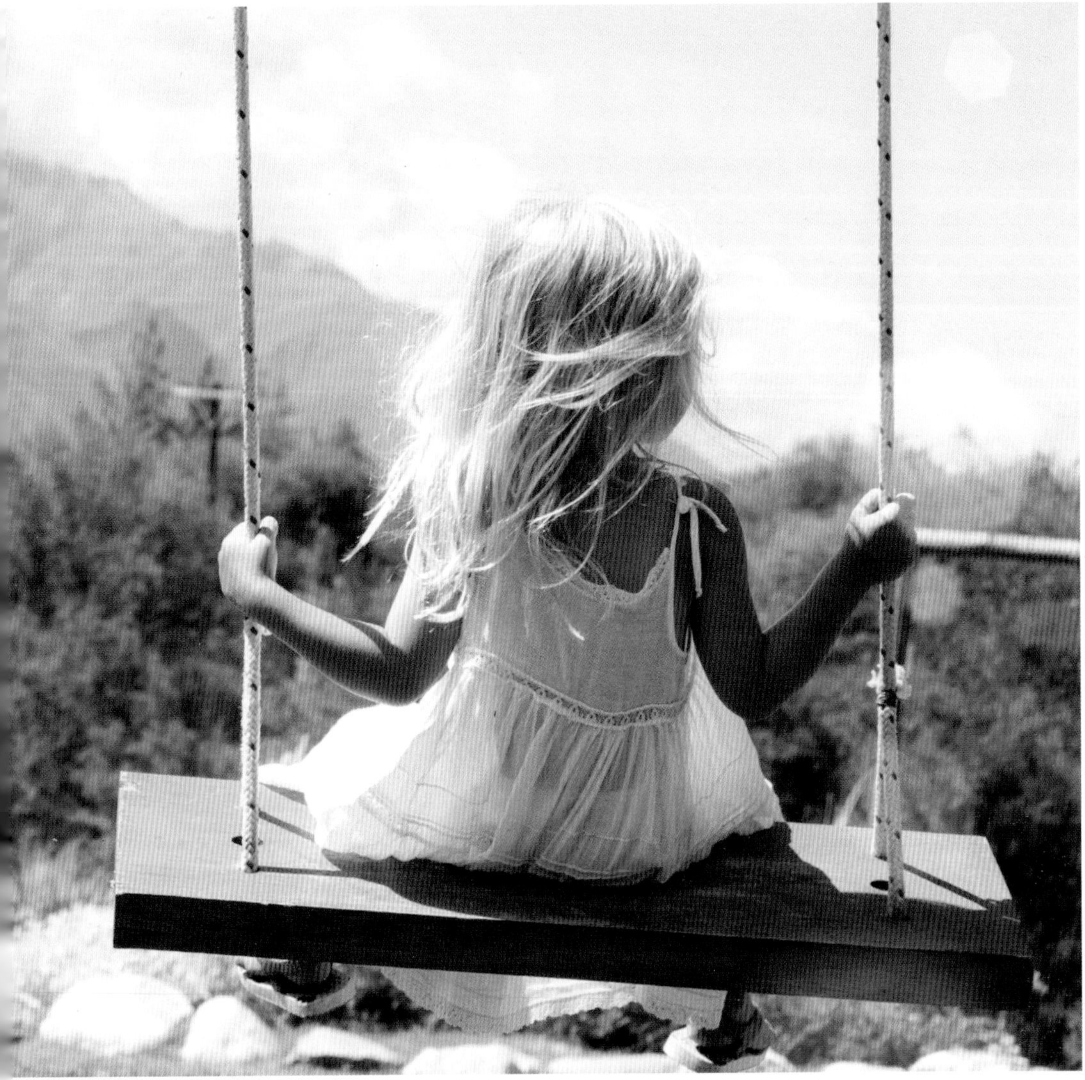

TIP 26
HAPPY MEDIUM

TOUCHY FEELY

Never underestimate the power of the human touch to create deep connection in your relationships. Literally physically connecting can create meaningful bonds - a mother with her baby, friends hugging, a firm handshake between business people, a pat on the back for a job well done, the gentle stroke of a loved one.

TIP #27

Physical touch touches our inner being and creates deep connections. Even if you wouldn't classify yourself as a *touchy feely* person, be more tactile and feel the difference.

SOULTISFY

Expressing our natural creativity is fundamental to our well-being.

Creativity helps us to express ourselves and gain self-awareness.

It can also increase our problem solving skills, relieve stress and when we

are in 'the zone' we lose track of time which can be mighty soultisfying.

TIP #28

Make creativity a habit in your life. Creative pursuits help you discover your innate

curiosity and as you continue to learn new resourceful ways of solving problems you

can then also apply these skills that you learn to different areas of your life.

BLISS ONESELF

They say that laughter is the best medicine. It can help you reduce stress levels rapidly, lower your blood pressure, boost your immune system, and trigger the release of endorphins which make you feel good all over.

TIP #29

Every day find a reason to bliss yourself laughing. Listen to a funny joke, watch a hilarious sitcom, take a look on the internet at the insanely silly things people get up to.

Laugh till you have tears in your eyes and let it wash away any stress and anxiety.

EXCREME

We have been told to contain our stress and find ways to manage it. Some of these methods include medication. A simple and effective, if not what some may call an *extreme* way, is to scream. An intense scream releases pent up tension, anxiety and energy. Often we hold onto things and this can cause us stress-related illnesses down the track. A really good scream can have a cathartic effect, instantly leaving us with a sense of peace.

TIP #30

Scream. Scream out every ounce of breath and pent up tension. Be a responsible screamer to avoid unwanted attention - go for an isolated walk in the countryside, turn up the radio or pour your lungs out into a pillow and feel the euphoria that follows.

TANEOUS

Be 'funtaneous'. Some of the greatest moments in life are when we throw caution to the wind and do something on impulse. If you are someone who has their life planned, throw a wrench in the works and have some fun. Planning has its place, but life was meant to be fun, so don't give up an opportunity when it presents itself to let your hair down and enjoy the moment.

TIP #31

Your life will not spontaneously combust if you let loose once in a while. Be impulsive sometimes. Break away from routine and you will discover new things. Do something silly that makes you laugh and takes you out of your comfort zone like skinny dipping. Be curious - try out the new cafe for lunch, or go for a drive and see where the road takes you.

PHONE SESH

In the busy lives we lead these days it isn't always possible to catch up as often as we would like with our friends. Online communication is great but it just isn't the same as having a good chat over the phone. Sometimes the subtleties of a phone conversation are lost in translation not to mention the energy and excitement you hear in their voice.

TIP #32

Surprise a friend you haven't connected with for sometime and have a good phone session.

The great thing about great friends is that it doesn't matter if you haven't spoken or caught up for ages as you always just pick up where you left off. Nothing beats a good phone sesh.

BE
HAVE

You will not always know how you will get to where you want to be

but by believing, you will take consistent actions to get there.

Our thoughts determine our actions and behaviors. Habits are the

consistent actions we take. Great habits follows great belief.

Belief will provide you with the right behaviors to have what you want.

When you are consistently *being* what you want to be you will *have* it.

TIP #33

Are your behaviors consistent with your beliefs? If not, take stock of what you truly believe.

Consciously change your behaviors and you are on the road to the success you want.

COME
PASSION

Have you ever had your car break down and a total stranger stopped to assist you? Or have you ever read or witnessed an accident and seen total strangers come to rescue those in need at the risk of their own lives?

You need not wait for dramatic circumstances to perform a random act of kindness. Helping total strangers and showing compassion can take us away from being self centered and totally change our perspective.

TIP #34

All around you there are countless opportunities to show kindness to total strangers.

Give your seat to someone on the bus, smile at strangers, buy a homeless person a meal.

Let kindness and compassion be your compass to creating joy in a stranger's life and yours.

PET THERAPY

The companionship of a pet can help you relieve stress and combat depression. Petting your cat or dog has a calming effect, and feeding, grooming and exercising your pet takes you away from your thoughts and into the present moment.

TIP #35

Pets give us unconditional love and many studies have shown the health benefits of having them in our lives. Looking after and caring for pets is great for our well-being.

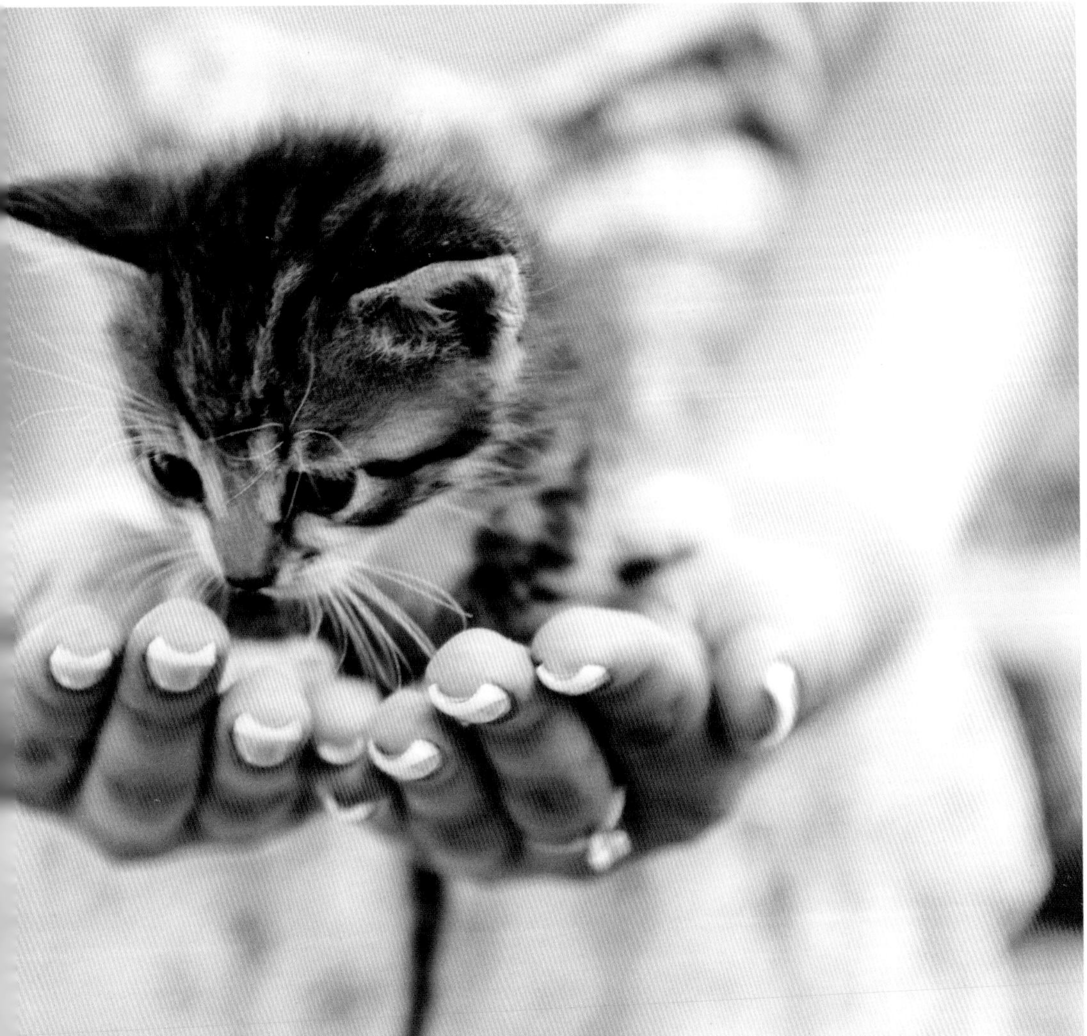

INTOMATE

We all like to imagine that the love of our life is also our best friend. However, the responsibilities and demands of life can sometimes take the spark out of many relationships. Our soul mate needs to not be just our best friend but our lover, and like anything in a relationship we need to make the time - time to be intimate. Intimacy lets them know that you are still into them.

TIP #36

Intimacy creates deep connection. The way your partner lovingly gazes into your eyes, the touch of their hand, that sensual kiss, the massage, the romantic gestures. Intimacy is much more than sexual connection. It is the little things you do to make love with each other every day that really counts. The little notes you leave, the way you speak and look at each other and the way you hold one another, help to nourish your mind, heart, body and soul.

SHOW
& TELL

Don't just tell someone you love them, let it show in
everything you do. Words are wonderful but actions really
do speak volumes. Don't just pay lip service to love, make it
show in everything you do.

TIP #37

We all want to feel nurtured by the loving care we receive from those around us.

Let them know in the little things you do - the cup of tea in the morning,

the wholesome meal you make or giving them the biggest piece of the pie.

MOTHER'S DAY

The bond between mother and daughter can often be the strongest that we may experience over our lifetime. When we are young our mother nourishes us and helps us grow, teaching us values and always being there for us. At times we can take our relationship for granted, expecting that is her parental duty. Never forget that your mother was once a child too and you have an opportunity to become lifelong friends.

TIP #38

Set aside time for *mother's day* - a day when you can regularly spend time with your mother and do things you both enjoy - go out shopping, watch a movie or make dinner together.

SUN DAY

It is important to take time off from our busy lives to nurture ourselves.

Sunday to many cultures is the day of rest. The word *sunday* literally

means *the day of the sun*. Contrary to many people's beliefs, moderate

exposure to sunlight is very beneficial to our physical health.

Sunlight can also have a therapeutic effect, relieving stress and

the symptoms of depression.

TIP #39

Schedule in a little sun in your day. Get up early and watch the sun rise, or catch up with

some friends after work for a sundowner and a sunset, or sit in the sun for a few minutes at

lunchtime and soak up the sun's rays. Let the calming effect of the sun make every day a *sun*day.

WILD
SIDE

Nature can teach us a lot about life and also about ourselves.

Deep within us lies an animal nature that society teaches us to keep at bay.

Adventurous activities help bring out the animal from within us.

TIP #40

Walk on the wild side and get in touch with your inner animal. Visit a zoo and experience the energy of lions and tigers, or for the adventurous, go behind the wheel of a racing car, take to the skies in a fighter jet, ride a horse or hop on board a roller coaster. Feel the adrenaline pump through your veins and let your spirit run free. High-power, high-adrenaline activities help us get in touch with parts of us we didn't know existed and understand that we are all wild at heart.

MOJO

There are times in our lives when our confidence takes a good hit.

They are the moments when it is easy to fall into a funk which we may find

difficult to climb out of. Life teaches us many lessons and those periods

when we are feeling down are not only good for reflecting on things but

they are also a time to ask for the help and support of those around us.

TIP #41

Never forget that there are people who love and care for you who can help you feel nurtured

and supported. With a little help you will again begin to feel your *mojo rising*.

Your *moments of joy*, or mojo will return as does your self confidence.

RISING

SATIATE

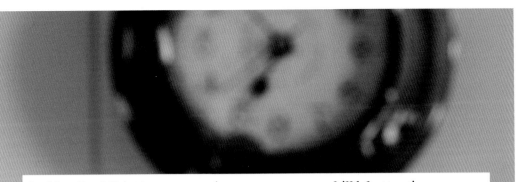

Sati is a Buddhist term meaning *awareness* or *skillful attentiveness.*

It is a present time awareness when we are doing something and we feel a sense of flow as we do it almost effortlessly. We aren't distracted by other things we need to do or remembering something in the past - we are totally present to this very moment. When we are in the flow it can fill us with great joy and nurture our soul.

TIP #42

A great way to get into the flow and feel sen*sati*onal is simply to NOT multi-task.

Instead focus on a single task. Be fully present when you make a cup of tea.

Give it your full attention. Let go of the urge to set a deadline. Instead immerse

yourself into the task and let your undivided attention transport you to *now*vana.

READ
ITATION

The benefits of reading books are mind blowing. Reading books provides mental stimulation, expands your vocabulary, helps you gain knowledge, improves your writing skills, focus and concentration and can help reduce stress as you get lost in a great story.

TIP #43

Read daily to feed your mind and nurture your soul. Set aside quiet time, it may be on the train to work or at bedtime. It helps you to be still and is perfect for those who find it hard to meditate as reading a good book requires focus not on your breathing but your reading.

You may say that reading can be a form of meditation we like to call *readitation*.

BOUNCE
ABILITY

How is your *bounceability?* Do you bounce back from life's challenges

or do you find it difficult to get up again. A person with resilience is

able to adapt quickly to changes and can maintain inner calm in

stressful situations. They also possess great humor and can laugh

at themselves and the situation much quicker and recover.

TIP #44

Become more resilient by looking at the positive lessons you can learn from the experience

and resist retreating into victim mode. Instead see how you can solve the problem rather than

be paralysed by negativity. Each challenge is an opportunity to increase your *bounceability.*

Negative self-talk can make our misery multiply like, well, rabbits. If we listen long enough to unsupportive, self-defeating, abusive and limiting statements, we can begin to believe them and they become our reality and the experiences we have in life. Some examples of negative thoughts include, I'm not good enough, I'm fat and ugly, nobody loves me, I'm undeserving, I'm stupid or I don't have enough time.

TIP #45

Every time you have a negative unsupportive thought instead of allowing it to kill your joy, neutralize it with two positive statements about yourself. Another great way to exterminate the little negativity bunnies is to write down positive affirmations and have them on your bathroom mirror so that you can start the day with affirmative positive thoughts.

HEAL
GOOD

Just like when we come down with the flu, we need time to rest and

recuperate to get better. The same goes when we are recovering from

some traumatic experience, whether it be a relationship break up,

the death of a loved one or any other circumstance.

TIP #46

Time does heal so remember to give yourself the space to heal, whether that means time to

grieve, time to mourn, time to heal good again. Don't put a time limit to your healing.

Everyone is different. Nurture yourself, seek the support of others and allow time to heal.

FACE

TIME

With modern technology it is so easy to live our lives almost

entirely through social media and electronic communications.

Communicating with others has become communEcating, where

emails and other electronic forms becomes the norm.

However we are humans, not computers, and nothing is quite like

catching up with friends for a coffee, and creating real life memories.

TIP #47

Schedule in regular face time (not Facebook time) to nurture your relationships.

Nothing is better for the heart and soul than face to face time with good friends.

FEEL
GRACE

Gratitude is all about focusing on the great things in your life.

Great things need not be *great big things*, and often, it is the

great little things that give us the greatest joy. If you want to

feel great try a little bit of gratitude.

TIP #48

Keep a gratitude diary and daily write down what you are truly grateful for in your life

right now. When you focus on the great things like your friends, family and your health,

you feel great more often. In fact, focusing on the good things in your life has a way

of attracting more goodness into it. Some call this goodness *luck*, others call it *grace* .

GROW UP

As a child did you ever do something that an adult said was silly and you were told to grow up? Maybe as an adult you were told that?

Don't ever grow up in the sense that you need to follow society's norms. This is your life. Don't ever lose your sense of curiosity and child-like wonder. Don't ever stop dreaming. It is OK to see things differently. Nurture your child-like spirit, let others grow old while you grow young.

TIP #49

As children we are told to stop being *nosey*. Don't listen. Children are naturally inquisitive.

Curiosity is vital for learning and gaining valuable skills. Curiosity *skilled* the cat. Try new things. Start a new hobby. Go learn a language at night school. Let your curiosity run free.

LOVE
IT UP

Don't ever do anything in life half-heartedly. Put your heart into it.

Whether it is vacuuming the house, finishing a report or commitments

you make. Passion is what gives life meaning. You are a heartist and

don't ever be afraid to make everything you do a work of heart.

TIP #50

You may have had your heart broken but never be afraid to wear your heart on your sleeve.

It will mend. Live a life of passion where everything you do creates joy. You can live your life

with either love or fear - the choice is yours. Don't let fear keep you down, love it up!

BIBLIOGRAPHY

Tip#05 http://www.jcf.org/new/index.php?categoryid=31

Tip#08 http://greatist.com/happiness/unexpected-health-benefits-music

Tip#29 http://life.gaiam.com/article/7-benefits-laughter

Tip#30 https://worldpulse.com/node/28602

Tip#42 http://www.vipassana.com/meditation/mindfulness_in_plain_english_15.php

Tip#44 http://www.sharecare.com/health/mental-health/what-are-benefits-resilience

Tip#45 http://thinksimplenow.com/happiness/negative-self-talk/

More inspiring titles by the authors:

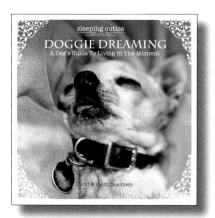